"A TALE OF SUPPLY AND DEMAND"

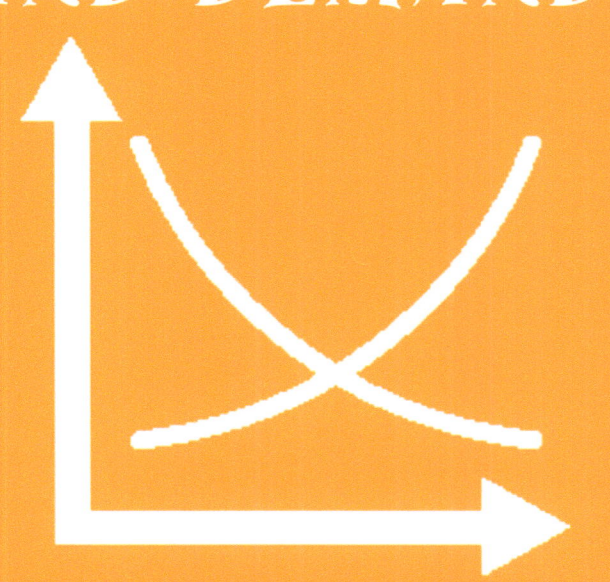

Once upon a sunny day,
Bunny craved a treat
He could not find a carrot,
So **demand**,
he could not meet.

So Bunny went to market,
But saw that even there,
A very small amount of carrots,
Were offered for the hare.

He then spoke to the storekeeper,
And with a fearful hunch,

Said:
"I will give you just one coin,
to satisfy my munch."

The storekeeper
looked at Bunny,
Frankly quite surprised,
"These carrots
are in high demand,
Their price will surely rise."

You see that line of bunnies,
Waiting quietly so nice?
They all want these few carrots,
And they will pay
any price!"

Bunny line
starts there...

So Bunny went outside to see,
And much to his dismay,

A crowd of many bunnies stood there,
Eager just to pay.

With bags of coins and gold galore,

Some even took a loan, To buy those
sweet, sweet carrots, **They so badly want to own....**

"But these are merely carrots"

Bunny quickly thought,
"This demand, it cannot last,
This bubble must be popped!"

So Bunny went back home, And in his heart, a pledge!
"To bring the carrot's price down now,
The economy is on edge!"

He worked and planted day by day,
And in his garden grew,

A never-before-seen amount of carrots,
Through and through.

Then Bunny rushed to market,
With a cart full of **supply**,

And presented such abundance,
For everyone to try.

Now every shop in Bunnyville, Was overfilled with stock,

And carrots were just everywhere,
The lines for them had stopped.

The town hall clock was ringing,
The time has come for lunch,

And Bunny,
with his lonely coin,
Can satisfy his munch.

8ᵀᴴ WONDER OF THE WORLD
(A tale of compound intrest)

Bunny sat in his cozy burrow, thinking:
"How can I save, So I won't have to borrow."
Saving a 'nest egg' is what I strive, to help me build a
comfortable life.

But what is the secret to saving I wonder?
I'll ask my friend **Owl-bert!**
So I won't have to ponder.

Owl-bert lived in the forest, In a big and ancient tree.
He was old and smart and wise,
And also, financially free.
Bunny asked owl,
Do let me know the trick,
How is it that your savings grow grater,
each passing week?

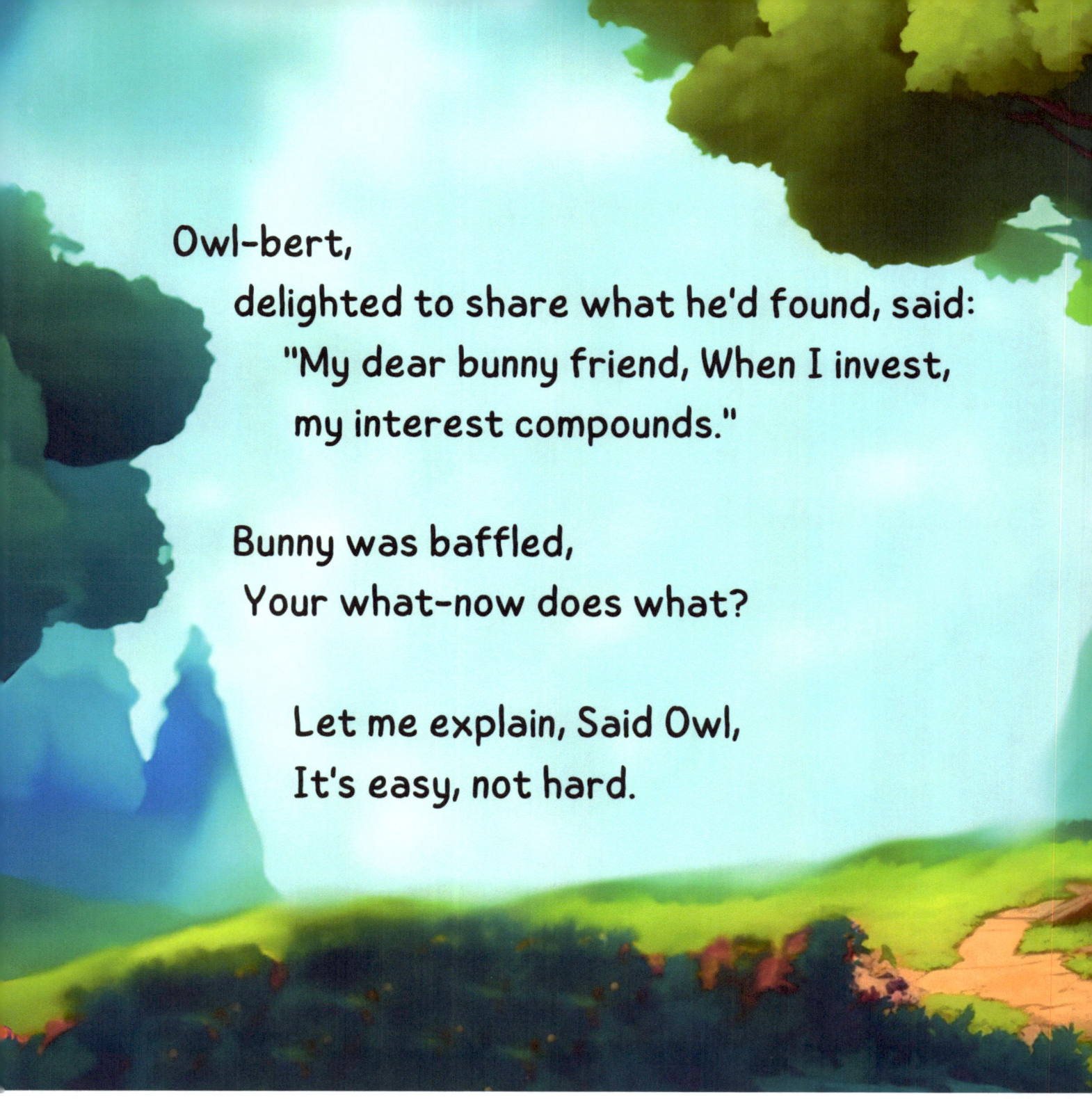

Owl-bert,
 delighted to share what he'd found, said:
  "My dear bunny friend, When I invest,
  my interest compounds."

Bunny was baffled,
 Your what-now does what?

  Let me explain, Said Owl,
  It's easy, not hard.

When you loan your coin, Say... to a friend in need.

It's like planting a forest, using just one seed.

Your friend will return your coin,

Without a doubt.

But they need to pay a bit extra,

To thank you for helping them out.

That extra coin of gratitude

"interest" is it's name,

The more you give, the more you get it.

It's part of the money game.

That's not much of a magic...
Said Bunny with a frown,
But wait! There's more! said Owl,
This is just where it gets fun!
Instead of using interest,
To buy a drink or snack – You lend it out again,
More intrest to collect.

And so that lonely coin you lend out to a friend,
is now worth 2 and 4 and more,
with basically no end.

I see, said Bunny,

With a twinkle in his eyes.

So **interest** is the "**thank you**"

And **compound** is the "**prize!**"

It's money making money

And growing bit by bit,

At first a little slow

But after many years so swift

So Bunny thanked dear Owl,
For his valuable advice.

And went to think of other
things, To compound in his life.

He strolled the ancient forest,
remembering Owl-bert's words.
(Who's last name's maybe... Owl-stein?)

On the power
of compound interest,
The 8th wonder of the world.

FINANCE -

Finance is all about how we use and manage our money. It's like playing a game where we earn, save, and spend our money wisely. When we save our money, it's like putting it in a special jar to keep it safe. We can use our saved money to buy things we need or want in the future, like toys or treats.

Finance helps us make smart choices about how we use our money, so we can have fun and be prepared for what we need.

What is 'SUPPLY & DEMAND' -

"Imagine you have a special toy that everyone wants to play with, but you only have a few of them. That means there is a limited supply of toys. Now, there are many friends who really want to play with your toy, so there is a big demand for it. When something is in high demand but there isn't enough of it, other kids might be willing to give you more things or even more money to get it. That's because the toy becomes very valuable when there isn't enough for everyone. so, supply is about how much of something there is, and demand is about how much other kids want it. When supply is low and demand is high, things can become very special and valuable!"

What is 'INTEREST' -

Remember the toys we talked about earlier in the page about supply and demand? Now, let's say your friend wants to borrow one them for a little while. When they return it, they will give you an extra toy as a thank you! That extra car is like interest. It's a little something extra you get when you lend or save something, like money, and it makes what you have even more. So, interest is like a special bonus that makes your saved or borrowed things grow over time.

COMPOUND INTEREST -

Compound interest is like a magical money-growing spell! When you save your money in a special place, it grows bigger and bigger over time. Not only does the money you put in grow, but the extra money you earn also starts to grow too! It's like a snowball rolling down a hill, getting bigger and bigger as it goes. So, the more you save and the longer you keep your money in that special place, the more it will grow. Compound interest is a wonderful way to make your money grow and help you achieve your dreams when you get older.